Clarence House

OFFICIAL SOUVENIR GUIDE

Contents

Introduction

Clarence House is the official London residence of Their Royal Highnesses The Prince of Wales, The Duchess of Cornwall and Prince Harry. The Prince of Wales uses the House to receive visitors from the United Kingdom and overseas and for official dinners, receptions and meetings. The House also provides offices for around 50 of His Royal Highness's official staff, who help to support his royal duties and charitable activities.

The Prince of Wales is the seventh royal occupant of Clarence House. His predecessors include the Duke of Clarence (later King William IV), for whom the House was built in the 1820s; Her Majesty The Queen and The Duke of Edinburgh from 1949 to 1952; and Her Late Majesty Queen Elizabeth The Queen Mother, whose home it was for half a century.

During 2002–03 the opportunity was taken to carry out long-awaited repairs to the House, which was then redecorated and refurnished for use by The Prince of Wales. The interiors now reflect His Royal Highness's requirements and taste, but at the same time incorporate almost all of the contents that were there in The Queen Mother's time.

For many years The Queen Mother encouraged visits to Clarence House by charities and organisations with which she was connected. The Prince of Wales has now greatly extended this more public use of the House by opening it to visitors during the summer months.

This new guidebook tells the story of Clarence House and its occupants, from 1827 to the present day. The principal rooms and their contents are described on pages 42–55.

Architectural History

JOHN NASH'S HOUSE

Clarence House was built between 1825 and 1827 to the designs of John Nash (1752–1835) as the London home of William, Duke of Clarence and his wife Adelaide. The new house incorporated the south-western corner of St James's Palace, which was originally built by Henry VIII between 1532 and 1540. Since the sixteenth century the Palace has accommodated not only the sovereign but princes, chiefly the eldest sons of monarchs, and royal dukes and their families. At the time Clarence House was built, the Dukes of York and Cumberland, two of George IV's brothers, and their sister Princess Augusta were living within the Palace's precincts, while another brother, the Duke of Clarence, had been living in a house at the western end of the Palace since 1789. His apartments had been redecorated and refurnished in the 1800s, but following his marriage in 1818, the Duke no longer regarded them as adequate. In 1824 he wrote to Sir William Knighton, Keeper of the Privy Purse:

His Majesty is fully aware of the inconvenience and unfitness of our present apartments here. They were arranged for me in 1809 when I was a bachelor, and without an idea at the time of my ever being married; since when (now 15 years) nothing has been done to them; and you well know the dirt and unfitness for the Duchess of our present abode. I earnestly request, for the sake of the amiable and excellent Duchess, you will ... represent [to the King] the wretched state and dirt of our apartments.

George IV was sympathetic.

The Duke of Clarence, accustomed by many years in the navy to the privations of life at sea, had tolerated on land rooms that were small, ill-connected and anything but princely. The task of transforming the Duke's quarters was given to John Nash, one of the 'attached' architects of the Board of Works with specific responsibility for St James's Palace.

ABOVE
Richard Cosway (1742–1821), *William, Duke of Clarence,* miniature, *c.*1795.

LEFT
The porch was added in the 1870s, when the South Front became the entrance front.

OPPOSITE
Looking south from inside the precinct of St James's Palace across Stable Yard Road towards the West Front of Clarence House, which was originally designed by Nash to be the entrance front.

Nash's plans for Clarence House (which do not survive) were submitted to the Board in March 1825. The outward appearance of St James's Palace, with its lengthy brickwork façades, disguises a continuous building history dating from the 1540s, and up until this point none of the architects of the different phases of building – Sir John Vanbrugh, Nicholas Hawksmoor or Nash himself in his rebuilding of the State Apartments from 1820 to 1824 – had departed from the Tudor language of brick and stone for the exterior. In his new proposal Nash did so emphatically, adding at one corner of the rambling Tudor pile a bright, stuccoed mansion of classical proportions.

As so often with Nash's buildings, the regularity of the façade obscured a great many complications. The pre-existing buildings (shown opposite) formed a row of houses facing on to what was then a public thoroughfare, Stable Yard Road. The Duke

LEFT
Detail from a survey plan of St James's Palace by T.J. Hunt, 1816, showing the Duke of Clarence's apartments (60, shaded blue) and the adjoining house occupied by Princess Augusta (61); the plan is presented with the Mall (lying to the south) shown at the top, and York House shown at the right.

of Clarence's old house adjoined the apartments of his sister, Princess Augusta, second daughter of George III.

In view of the complicated history of the existing buildings, Nash's original estimate

JOHN NASH

Nash (1752–1835) had been appointed one of the Surveyors-General of the Board of Works in 1813, at the age of 61, after a successful career as a country-house architect in partnership with the landscape gardener Humphrey Repton. He became one of George IV's favourite architects, creating Brighton Pavilion for him in 1815 and radically re-ordering the area north of St James's Park to form Regent Street and Regent's Park. He was also responsible for the remodelling of Buckingham House into Buckingham Palace for the King, but his career came to an abrupt end on George IV's death in 1830.

ABOVE
Joseph Nash (1808–78), *Buckingham Palace: the East Front as completed, with the Marble Arch at the centre of the forecourt*, watercolour, 1846.

that his proposals would cost between £9,000 and £10,000 was hopelessly unrealistic. After the demolition of much of the old house, the condition of what was left was found to be very poor. The material of the wall adjoining Princess Augusta's house was, in the architect's words, 'little better than rubbish', and other walls required underpinning because their foundations would have been inadequate for the building now proposed.

This sort of additional expense was perhaps to be expected when dealing with ancient and much altered buildings, but what gave the Surveyor-General of the Board of Works and the Treasury greater cause for complaint were the numerous alterations to the original plan which Nash made as work proceeded. In September 1826 Nash was called to account for the fact that the building had grown one metre in height since the designs were approved, and dormer windows had been built and then removed. The architect replied that he had raised the height of the attic on learning that some of the rooms 'were to be appropriated as Sitting Rooms to the Ladies they being in their original state too low for Apartments so occupied', adding that the dormers 'appeared so prominent a feature over the Balcony that I ordered them to be removed'. The final total cost, after fitting-out was completed at the beginning of 1829, was calculated at £22,232.

ABOVE
The West Front seen from across Stable Yard; Nash's classical design for Clarence House forms a marked contrast to the older brick façade of the adjoining St James's Palace.

OPPOSITE
Joseph Nash, *Clarence House, the South Front*, watercolour, 1851. On the far left is York House (subsequently Stafford House and now Lancaster House), which was built for Clarence's elder brother, the Duke of York.

Though more than twice the initial estimate, that figure was still extremely modest when compared with the outlay on building expended on behalf of the Duke of Clarence's two elder brothers. While Clarence House was being built, Frederick Augustus, the 'Grand Old' Duke of York and retired Commander-in-Chief of the British army, was constructing his own, much larger, house (now Lancaster House) on the south side of Stable Yard. Referring to the simultaneous construction of Buckingham Palace, for George IV, and York House, the MP Thomas Creevey wrote in his diary for September 1826:

To think of these two men ... both turned sixty, and terrible bad lives, having new palaces building for them! The Duke of York's is 150 ft by 130 ft outside, with forty compleat sleeping apartments, and all this for a single man ... Billy Clarence, too, is rigging up in a small way in the Stable Yard, but that is doing by the Government.

The appearance of the new house is recorded in Victorian photographs and on a block plan of St James's Palace made in 1841 (see p. 12). It had three storeys above a basement and was still arranged to face Stable Yard Road. A double entrance portico at the centre of the new West Front led to the Entrance Hall (now the Library), which in turn connected with a long corridor or gallery running the whole width of the house parallel to the road.

The interior of Clarence House was plain in comparison to those at Buckingham Palace and York House. Ornamental plasterwork was confined to the reception rooms on the first floor, where Francis Bernasconi (1762–1841), who also worked for George IV at Buckingham Palace, decorated the fluted coves of the ceilings with slender sprays of foliage. These rooms were hung with crimson damask. For the furnishings, solid mahogany was preferred to gilded wood – indeed, the Duke of Clarence seems to have had an aversion to gilding, an isolated instance in his generation of the royal family.

The Duke's only subsequent addition to the House arose from his decision to remain there after having succeeded to the throne, as William IV, in 1830. This was the creation of a first-floor passage from the new House to connect with the State Apartments in St James's Palace, where he would conduct his official audiences and receive guests. It was designed by Sydney Smirke and passed over the Palace carpenters' shop on the ground floor.

ABOVE
Clarence House, photographed *c.*1861: the South Front, facing the garden.

RIGHT
In the late 1830s the buildings to the south of Clarence House were demolished, forming the open area that is now the garden.

BELOW
Detail from the plan of St James's Palace, made in 1841 and laid out with south at the top, showing (on the right) the ground floor of Nash's house, with the hall and portico opening on to Stable Yard, and (at the top) the conservatory and porch added by the Duchess of Kent .

OPPOSITE
Clarence House and the garden today, showing how Waller's design made the South Front appear continuous with that of St James's Palace.

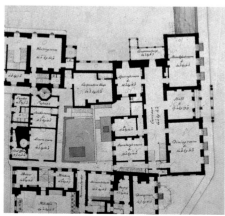

After William IV's death in 1837, Clarence House became the home of his unmarried sister (and former next-door neighbour) Princess Augusta, until her death in 1840. During this time the Princess's old house, which was attached to Clarence House on the south side, and the remaining buildings beyond it were demolished, opening the House to the enclosed garden of St James's Palace to the south.

The next occupant of the House, Queen Victoria's mother, the Duchess of Kent, took advantage of these demolitions by making a door at the south end of the ground-floor corridor, enabling her to enter and leave the House from the Mall without having to use the still-public Stable Yard Road. The plan of St James's Palace made in 1841 (see left), the year the Duchess moved in, and Joseph Nash's watercolour of 1851 (see p. 10) show the small conservatory she built against the south side of the House as a new entrance hall, with a porch projecting from one end. The porch had been designed with retracting screens, to enable the Duchess to cross the pavement outside her former home, Ingestre House (36 Belgrave Square), to her carriage without being observed. It was moved to Clarence House at a cost of £175.

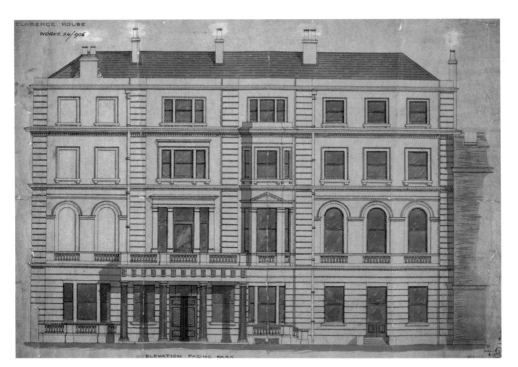

Meanwhile the passage connecting Clarence House with the State Apartments in the Palace was adapted to accommodate the Duchess's wardrobe, and the former carpenters' shop below it was incorporated in the ground floor of Clarence House, as an office for her Clerk of Accounts. The rooms were redecorated with pale painted papers, replacing the now distressed damask hangings, which were considered too dark. Gilding was introduced on the mouldings of the Drawing Rooms and Dining Room, again with the intention of making them appear lighter (probably the last work of the gilder Edward Wyatt, 1757–1833, who had worked for both George III and George IV).

The appearance of the House in the Duchess of Kent's time is recorded in a series of watercolours in the Royal Library (see p. 27). In the first-floor drawing rooms, the Duke of Clarence's damask curtains were replaced in chintz, and the watercolours also show the suites of rosewood furniture covered in chintz and silk and wool damask supplied for the Duchess's use through the Office of Woods and Forests.

The reorientation of the House towards the south was completed in the 1870s by its next occupant, Queen Victoria's second son, Alfred, Duke of Edinburgh, who employed the firm of Waller & Sons to fill in the gap between the projecting bay of the Duke of Clarence's House and the end of the State Apartments of the Palace, so that the House appeared as a continuation of the Palace's South Front. This now became the entrance front, centred on a *porte cochère* of fluted cast-iron Doric columns. Thomas Waller had been 'confidential clerk' to builder and developer Thomas Cubitt (1788–1855). As the main contractor for the laying-out of the

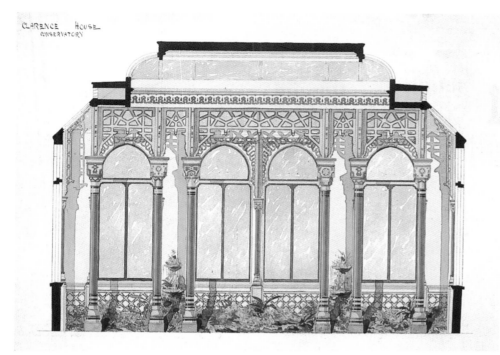

CLARENCE HOUSE
CONSERVATORY

THE RUSSIAN ORTHODOX CHAPEL

The most remarkable of all the new interiors designed by C.B. Waller was the Russian Orthodox Chapel, which was installed on the first floor of Clarence House for the Russian-born Duchess of Edinburgh. The Duchess's household included a Russian priest and chanter who officiated daily. Here Waller stretched the limits of his imagination to conjure up 'Russian' mouldings for the door surrounds. The Chapel was dismantled after the Duchess's departure, following her husband's death in 1900.

LEFT
The interior of the conservatory built above the porch on the South Front. With its brightly coloured columns, mosaic floor, carpets and 'ottoman' furnishings, it was the counterpart of the 'Turkish' smoking room designed for the Prince of Wales by Carl Haag and installed at Marlborough House.

Duke of Westminster's London estate, Cubitt had been responsible for the propagation of the Nash style in the painted stucco terraces, squares and mansions of Belgravia, as well as for the building of Osborne House on the Isle of Wight and the new Ballroom at Buckingham Palace. Thomas Waller's son Robert John Waller took over Cubitt's firm in 1856. The Clarence House improvements were designed and directed by his eldest son, Charles Bullen Waller.

The remodelling of the House was occasioned by the Duke's marriage in 1874, in the Winter Palace at St Petersburg, to the daughter of Tsar Alexander II of Russia, the Grand Duchess Marie Alexandrovna, to whom even the enlarged Clarence House must have seemed modest. As a younger son of the sovereign, the Duke had to pay for the improvements himself, with only the eradication of rot and sanitary improvements being considered a charge on the Office of Works.

If C.B. Waller's new South Front was entirely conservative, his designs for the interior were more progressive, even fashionable. Nash's corridors became 'Old English' long galleries, with geometric plaster ceilings, oak dados and doorcases, and the stairs were given corresponding turned oak balustrades. The former Breakfast Room (now the Morning Room) was given an 'Aesthetic' new look, with a stencilled ceiling and cove, foliate-patterned wallpaper and stuffed seat furniture covered in matching patterned velvet (see left). When the Queen's Private Secretary, Henry Ponsonby, was shown this room just after its completion in 1876, he pronounced it 'pretty' and 'medoeval', adding somewhat wearily that it also appeared expensive. Upstairs, oriental overtones became the main theme. At the south end of the first-floor corridor a 'Japanese' fretwork glazed screen gave into a conservatory of a decidedly 'Moorish' character, built on top of the *porte cochère*.

The next occupants of the House, the Duke and Duchess of Connaught, moved in after redecorations had been carried out in 1901. They made several changes to the principal rooms, removing the partition between the two first-floor drawing rooms to make one large room, and introducing decorative plasterwork in the style of Robert Adam in the Dining Room. In 1914 the conservatory over the *porte cochère* was adapted as a sitting room for the invalid Duchess, involving the removal of all the original glazing. The whole structure was dismantled in 1948.

The Duke and Duchess (her health permitting) were abroad for much of the time that Clarence House was theirs, and from his retirement until his death in 1942, the Duke made no further architectural changes.

TOP
This contemporary photograph shows the Hall in Alfred, Duke of Edinburgh's time.

ABOVE
The Morning Room in Alfred, Duke of Edinburgh's time.

OPPOSITE
The Morning Room as it looks today.

BELOW
This view from the Library through to the Morning Room shows one of the two new double doorways made in the 1950s, the other opening from the Library into the Dining Room, to form an interconnected suite of rooms.

When it was decided that the House should become the London home of Princess Elizabeth and Philip, Duke of Edinburgh, after their marriage in 1947, it required complete renovation. The electric wiring and the heating and hot-water systems were modified versions of what had been laid on in 1874 and, though there were six baths in the House, only one was in a room reserved for its use – the others were in dressing rooms. The renovations, which cost £55,000, included the repair of wartime bomb damage to the roof, and the interconnection of Clarence House with the earlier house immediately to the north for the offices of the Duke and Duchess's household.

When Queen Elizabeth The Queen Mother moved into Clarence House in May 1953, she reinstated the Duke's study as her Morning Room, installing a Georgian marble chimneypiece and a new plaster ceiling with her own crown flanked by palm fronds in relief at either end. A new double

doorway was created at the north end of the room to connect with the Library, from where another door linked to the Dining Room beyond, making for easier circulation when the House was full of guests.

Queen Elizabeth's only other major change to the House was the removal of a partition to create the Garden Room from two rooms in 1960. In the decoration of the House Queen Elizabeth was advised over many years by Oliver Ford, who worked for the long-established London firm of Lenygon & Morant and later founded his own business. In his periodic renewal of upholstery fabrics and paint schemes, the light and airy character established during the 1940s renovation was maintained.

In 2002–03, in order to prepare the House as the London residence of The Prince of Wales, the decorator and interior designer Robert Kime (who holds His Royal Highness's warrant) renewed the decorations in all the principal rooms. Drawing on his experience of working at Highgrove and The Prince of Wales's former apartments at St James's, he took the opportunity to adjust the colour schemes in most rooms while introducing a greater variety of textiles, including some richly patterned oriental fabrics, for curtains and upholstery.

While the arrangement of the rooms and the grouping of their contents remain much as in Queen Elizabeth's time, with many works of art from Her Majesty's collection in the same positions, several pieces from elsewhere in the Royal Collection and from The Prince of Wales's own collection have been introduced to give new accents and highlights. These alterations are designed to reflect the change of occupancy while at the same time maintaining the familiar atmosphere of a much-loved family house.

HRH THE DUKE OF EDINBURGH'S STUDY IN 1949

After the House became the London home of Princess Elizabeth and HRH The Duke of Edinburgh in 1947, the Victorian interiors were entirely swept away and everything was done to give the newly married couple as bright and clean a house as possible. The Duke of Edinburgh took overall charge of the work, while Princess Elizabeth selected the paint colours for the principal rooms. The work was carried out against the background of post-war restrictions on building and materials, and the completed interiors were remarkable for their simplicity and absence of luxury. The white maplewood panelling and furniture in the Duke's study (now the Morning Room) were manufactured in Toronto as a wedding present from the Canadian Pacific Railway Company.

ABOVE HRH The Duke of Edinburgh's study (now the Morning Room) in 1949.

The Occupants of Clarence House

WILLIAM, DUKE OF CLARENCE AND ST ANDREWS (1827–1837)

BELOW
Johann Zoffany (1733–1810), *King George III, Queen Charlotte and their six eldest children*, oil on canvas, 1770. This family portrait shows the princes George, Prince of Wales (later George IV), Frederick, Duke of York, William, Duke of Clarence, and Edward, Duke of Kent (Queen Victoria's father), with their sisters Charlotte and Augusta.

William Henry, third son of George III and Queen Charlotte, was born at Buckingham House on 21 August 1765. Brought up at Kew with his younger brother Prince Edward, later Duke of Kent (Queen Victoria's father), he was sent to sea as an able seaman at the age of 14, and served in the Royal Navy for 30 years before becoming an Admiral of the Fleet in 1811. Thereafter he was propelled gradually closer to the throne by a series of unexpected circumstances. His short reign (1830–37), though often overlooked – falling as it did between those of his flamboyant elder brother George IV and his niece Queen Victoria – saw the passage of the Great Reform Bill of 1832, the most important constitutional change for 200 years.

George III designed the education of his three eldest sons precisely with their future roles in mind. As his heir, Prince George Augustus Frederick, Prince of Wales, was not allowed to travel abroad or to serve in the armed forces. Prince Frederick, Duke of York, the next in line, entered the army and was sent to live in Germany between the ages of 18 and 25. The King's decision to send Prince William into the navy was made during the review of the fleet at Spithead in 1778. Such a choice was common for younger sons of aristocratic families, and among the King's motives must have been the likely beneficial effects of naval discipline, and the example of service to the nation at a time of international uncertainty brought about by the American Revolution and war in Europe.

From the outset the Prince revelled in his life at sea and found favour with his commanders, among whom was his friend and hero Captain Horatio Nelson. The Duke saw action in the Channel, in the West Indies and in the campaign against the rebel colonists in America. In New York in 1781 he was the object of a failed kidnap attempt sanctioned in person by General Washington. Although accompanied on

OPPOSITE
The Queen, her eldest son The Prince of Wales, and his oldest son Prince William, photographed in 2003 at Clarence House before a dinner to mark the 50th anniversary of the Coronation. Clarence House was home to the then Princess Elizabeth and her husband, Philip, Duke of Edinburgh, before her accession, and remains the official London home of Prince Charles.

board ship by carefully selected tutors, to his parents' distress the Prince enjoyed on land a series of bawdy adventures to rival those of his elder brothers.

When he was 17 the Prince was taken out of the navy for two years and sent to Hanover, to learn languages and, his parents hoped, manners. Impatient to return to sea, he was granted a commission as a lieutenant in 1785, serving on the Antigua station. The senior officer there was Nelson, who wrote approvingly of his royal subordinate.

In 1789, the year of the French Revolution and of his father's first serious bout of porphyria, Prince William was given his own establishment and an annual income of £18,000, with the titles of Earl of Munster and Duke of Clarence and St Andrews. Around 1790, having failed to secure his father's consent to his intended marriage to

RIGHT
Sir Thomas Lawrence (1769–1830), *William, Duke of Clarence*, 1827.

PRINCE WILLIAM & NELSON

John Hoppner (1758–1810), *Horatio, 1st Viscount Nelson (1758–1805)*, oil on canvas, 1801–02. Prince William served under Nelson on the Antigua station. Nelson wrote of the Prince: 'he has his foibles ... but they are far overbalanced by his virtues. In his professional line he is superior to nearly two thirds, I am sure, of the list: and in attention to orders and respect to his superior officers I hardly know his equal.' When Nelson married Mrs Fanny Nisbet in 1787 the Prince was his best man, but in an age when advancement in the Royal Navy was dependent on patronage, the commanding officer's view may have been somewhat coloured by the possibilities the Prince's friendship might bring in this direction. In the opinion of a fellow officer on board the *Pegasus*, the Prince was 'deficient in almost all the qualities necessary for a person in high command'.

the daughter of a retired naval captain and Commissioner of Portsmouth Dockyard, the Prince came under the spell of the greatest comic actress of the day. Dorothy (or Dora) Bland, known professionally as Mrs Jordan, was then the mistress of the connoisseur and collector Richard Ford. Mrs Jordan's ability to conquer the hearts of male audiences was memorably described by the diarist William Hazlitt:

There was no one else like her. Her face, her tones, her manner, were irresistible. Her smile had the effect of sunshine and her laugh did one good to hear it ... She was Cleopatra turned into an oyster-wench, without knowing that she was Cleopatra, or caring that she was an oyster-wench.

With the King's withdrawal to Windsor after the final onset of his madness in 1810, and the appointment of the Prince of Wales as Regent in the following year, a degree of respectability was urgently required on the part of the royal dukes and the question of the succession was brought into sharper focus. Only the Regent, his daughter Princess Charlotte and the Duke of York stood between the Duke of Clarence and the throne. Aware that his allowance as a married man would be more than double what he had as a bachelor, and that marriage to Mrs Jordan was out of the question, the Duke embarked on a seven-year search for a suitable bride.

In the end the choice fell on Princess Adelaide Louisa Thérèse Caroline, daughter of the Duke of Saxe-Meiningen, who at 25 was less than half the Duke's age. Speaking in a heated House of Commons debate on allowances for the increasingly indebted royal dukes, the future Prime Minister George Canning declared:

The Duke of Clarence would not have thought of contracting this marriage ... if it had not been pressed upon him as an act of public duty ... He contracted this alliance not for his own private gratification, but because he had been advised to do so for the politic purpose of providing for the succession to the throne ...

The Duke's duty had become more urgent after the death in November 1817 of the Prince Regent's only child, Princess Charlotte of Wales, shortly after giving birth to a stillborn son, a national tragedy that carried off two generations of the royal succession. In 1820, with the deaths of George III and the Duke of Kent, and with his eldest brother now installed on the throne, the Duke of Clarence petitioned for the improvement of his quarters at St James's, and in 1825 plans were prepared for the construction of the present Clarence House.

MRS JORDAN

From 1790 until 1811 the Duke and Mrs Jordan lived together effectively as man and wife. Already the mother of a child by the theatrical manager Richard Daly and of three by Richard Ford, Dora bore the Duke ten more children between 1794 and 1807, all of whom, unusually for the time, survived infancy. Though illegitimate and therefore excluded from the succession, they were given the surname Fitzclarence and several of them rose to prominent positions in the forces and in other areas of public life during the Victorian period. The Duke and Mrs Jordan lived in the apartments at St James's which had been made available to the Duke in 1789. From 1797, when he was appointed Ranger of Bushy Park (adjoining Hampton Court), they occupied the country house that went with the position. Finally, in 1811, as he drew closer to the succession, the Duke dismissed Mrs Jordan in order to make a dynastic marriage.

William IV desired this marble statue of Mrs Jordan to be erected 'beside the monument of the Queens' in Westminster Abbey. The Dean of Westminster refused to allow the finished statue into the Abbey, however, and for years it remained in Chantrey's studio, before passing down in the possession of Mrs Jordan's descendants. The statue was presented to The Queen by the Earl of Munster in 1975, and is now in Buckingham Palace.

LEFT
Sir Francis Chantrey (1781–1841), *Mrs Jordan*, marble statue (detail), 1834.

When George IV died in 1830, the Duke succeeded as King William IV at the age of 64. Although the ceremonial office of Lord High Admiral had recently been revived for him, he had played little part in public life. Nothing had prepared him for the throne, and few of his subjects had any idea what he looked like. Wandering up St James's Street in plain clothes a few days after holding his first Council as King, he was bundled into White's Club by a group of members who recognised their Sovereign in the street. His earliest biographer, Robert Huish, wrote that the new King had:

A perfect contempt for the arts of the courtier … he carried with him to the throne none of those assumptions, which are put on to elevate the monarch above the man but that really produce the opposite effect.

On his death George IV left the vastly extended Buckingham Palace far from complete, and the new King resolved to stay in his new house at St James's, adding the corridor at first-floor level to connect with the State Apartments. Clarence House was remarkably plainly decorated and furnished, and indeed William IV showed no more taste for the arts as King than he had as Duke. Confronted by one of his brother's outstanding Old Master pictures he remarked, 'Aye, it seems pretty – I dare say it is. My brother was fond of this sort of nick-nackery.'

Among George IV's other legacies were thousands of unsigned official documents, to which William IV dutifully applied himself. His first Prime Minister, the Duke of Wellington, remarked that he 'had done more business with him in ten minutes than with the other in ten days'. While the King struggled with the immense constitutional challenges posed by the Reform movement, his sister-in-law Victoria, Duchess of Kent, travelled around the country with her daughter Victoria, whom she introduced wherever they went as 'your future Queen'. Though he doted on his young niece and heir, William IV had never liked her mother and found this repeated intimation of his own mortality extremely tiresome. When he died in June 1837, the Princess had just passed her 18th birthday.

FAR LEFT
Mary Green (1776–1846) *Queen Adelaide*, miniature, 1821. The Duke of Clarence and Princess Adelaide were married on 13 July 1818 at Kew Palace, in a joint ceremony with the Duke of Kent and Princess Victoria of Saxe-Coburg-Saalfeld. The Duke and Duchess of Clarence lived initially in Hanover, where a child was born in March 1819, surviving for only a day. In 1820 they settled into Bushy Park, where the Duchess adapted with remarkable equanimity to a house full of Mrs Jordan's children.

LEFT
William Scoular (1796–1854), *Princess Elizabeth of Clarence*, 1821. The Clarences' second child died at the age of three months.

VICTORIA, DUCHESS OF KENT (1841–1861)

On 13 July 1837 Queen Victoria, accompanied by her mother the Duchess of Kent, drove in state from her childhood home, Kensington Palace, to Buckingham Palace. From this time the widowed Queen Adelaide lived for the most part at Bushy, with Marlborough House as her London residence. The vacant Clarence House was allocated to Princess Augusta, whose former house adjoining Clarence House was now demolished. After the death of William IV the crowns of Great Britain and Hanover were divided, because the laws of the latter kingdom allowed female sovereigns only if there was no male in line. The Queen's uncle, the Duke of Cumberland, succeeded to Hanover and his former apartments at St James's were allocated to her mother. The Duke took longer than expected to move out, however, and a house in Belgrave Square belonging to Viscount Ingestre, later 18th Earl of Shrewsbury, was taken for the Duchess of Kent as a temporary measure. By the time the Cumberland apartments were vacant, Princess Augusta had died and, Clarence House being once again available, it was decided that the Duchess should have it as her residence.

Having been widowed again within two years of her second marriage, the Duchess of Kent had raised and educated her daughter single-handedly. In this task she had depended on her brother Prince Leopold, who had married Princess Charlotte of Wales in 1816 and had been left a widower by the tragic events of November 1817. Leopold was later to introduce his niece Victoria to his nephew, Prince Albert. Intensely protective of her daughter, the Duchess often showed a tendency to steal her limelight, and her proud countenance can always be seen to the fore in Sir George Hayter's canvases of the ceremonial events of the early years of Queen Victoria's reign. In later life she turned her attentions increasingly to her grandchildren, one of whom, Queen Victoria's third son Arthur, Duke of Connaught (a future occupant of Clarence House), later recalled:

My sisters and I used to drive over from Buckingham Palace to Clarence House … in a 'town coach' with a coachman sitting on a Hammer Cloth, and two footmen standing up behind … Our Grandmother … was always very dear & kind, & spoilt us all. She used always to have some chocolates or little cakes for us when we visited her.

The Duchess's death, in the fatal year of 1861 which would also carry off the Prince Consort, left the Queen distraught. Before any of her mother's former rooms at Clarence House were touched, she had their appearance recorded in watercolours by James Roberts.

ABOVE
James Roberts (fl. 1775–1800), *The Drawing Room*, watercolour, 1861. These two paintings were part of a series commissioned by Queen Victoria after her mother the Duchess of Kent's death.

BELOW
James Roberts (fl. 1775–1800), *The Dining Room*, watercolour, 1861.

ALFRED, DUKE OF EDINBURGH (1866–1900)

Clarence House was left vacant for five years until 1866, when it was allocated to Queen Victoria's second son, Alfred Ernest Albert (1844–1900), created Duke of Edinburgh in the same year. Prince Alfred, known as 'Affie', had been born at Windsor Castle in 1844. His education and that of his elder brother Albert Edward ('Bertie'), Prince of Wales, the future King Edward VII, was placed in the hands of Baron Stockmar, who had been their father's tutor. It was Prince Albert's declared wish that, as heir and heir presumptive, their upbringing should be as 'unlike as possible [that of] their maternal great uncles', George IV and William IV. Should anything happen to the Prince of Wales, Affie would succeed Queen Victoria, and from an early age it was envisaged that, should Bertie survive his mother, Affie would inherit the Dukedom of Saxe-Coburg and Gotha from his uncle, Prince Albert's elder brother Duke Ernest.

Affie's keen childhood interests in geography and the sea, encouraged at Osborne, his parents' home on the Isle of Wight, made him ambitious to pursue a career in the navy, which his father decided would make him 'more generally competent' for either of his possible future roles. After initial training he joined HMS *Euryalus* as a midshipman in 1858. Like the Duke of Clarence, he was to rise to the rank of Admiral in the course of a 40-year career.

His first command, HMS *Galatea*, was engaged between 1866 and 1868 on two extensive tours, the first to Brazil and Australia. Having returned to Portsmouth in June 1867 laden with the gifts and trophies, the *Galatea* set out once more the following November. This time the route was to take in Fiji, Hawaii, New Zealand, Japan and India, a royal tour of unprecedented extent. In Japan, which for some 200 years had been almost completely inaccessible to Westerners, the Prince was received by the Emperor Meiji and presented with gifts including a full set of samurai armour (see p. 32), numerous weapons, and ornamental goods in lacquer, bronze and porcelain. Arriving at Calcutta in December 1869, the Prince embarked on a three-month tour of India as the guest of the Viceroy, Lord Mayo. This tour anticipated the even more extensive visit by the Prince of Wales in 1875–6, which in turn laid the foundations for Queen Victoria's proclamation as Empress and yielded a further quantity of exotic gifts.

A ROYAL DUKE

The Duke's first extensive naval tour, in 1866–7, was undertaken more in his capacity as a royal duke than for any reasons of naval deployment. He paid a state visit on his mother's behalf to the Emperor of Brazil, then sailed for Australia via the Cape. At all stages in the tour the Prince performed official ceremonies in Queen Victoria's name, laying the foundation stones of churches, town halls and harbours, and was presented with many gifts, both for himself and for the Queen.

LEFT J.E. Boehm (1834–1890), *Alfred, Duke of Edinburgh*, marble bust, 1879.

BELOW
Sectional drawing by the builder C.B. Waller, 1873, showing the proposed arrangement of pictures in the corridors. Waller was responsible for carrying out the improvements to the House commissioned by the Duke in the 1870s.

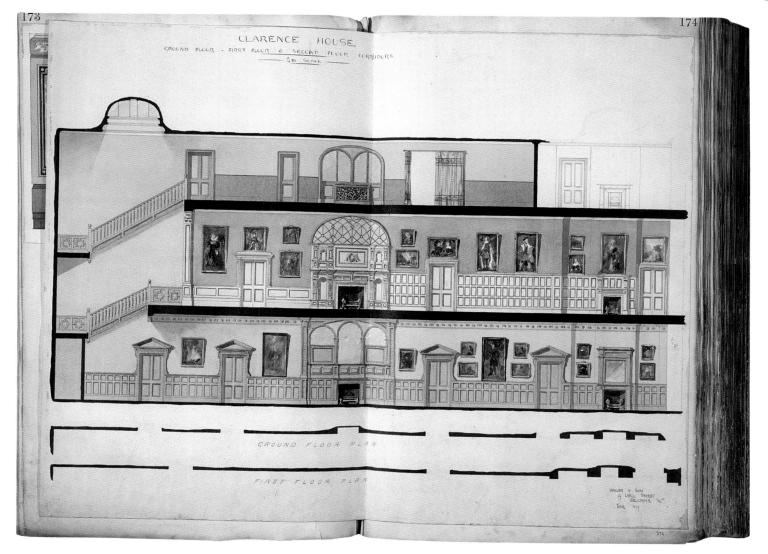

CLARENCE HOUSE
GROUND FLOOR · FIRST FLOOR & SECOND FLOOR CORRIDORS
¼ IN SCALE

GROUND FLOOR PLAN

FIRST FLOOR PLAN

In 1874 Prince Alfred was married in St Petersburg to the daughter of Tsar Alexander II, the Grand Duchess Marie Alexandrovna, and after his marriage he was allocated a further £10,000 a year, bringing his income to £25,000. He applied his new resources to the enlargement and decoration of Clarence House, including the creation of the Russian Orthodox chapel on the first floor (see p. 15). The new rooms were fitted out and decorated in a mixture of 'Old English' and more eclectic styles bordering on the Aesthetic, and the exotic note was enhanced by the display, on fitted overmantel shelves in the corridors and principal rooms, of the oriental porcelain, bronzes, lacquers and jades that the Prince had acquired on his travels. A catalogue of his possessions dating from the 1870s lists over 400 such pieces, including a large Japanese bronze incense burner presented by the Emperor, ivory carvings including netsuke, enamels, and Indian metalwork. Apart from a group of mounted coconut cups and other standing cups in silver gilt there was very little Western art of note. The few paintings were nearly all portraits lent by Queen Victoria, interspersed with 'souvenir' views of the Duke's travels and a large group of marine watercolours. In the large Drawing Room on the first floor the walls were a forest of oriental arms, shields and ceremonial staves.

When Affie's uncle Duke Ernest of Saxe-Coburg died in 1893, the Duke and Duchess of Edinburgh were forced to embark on a new life in Germany with their

five children. Parliament ruled that the Duke's income from the Civil List could not be expended in Germany, but he was allowed £10,000 annually for the upkeep of Clarence House, which he was determined to retain despite having now to reside for most of the year in Coburg, in a house opposite the Ducal Palace known as Palais Edinburgh.

Taken in all its aspects, the life of the Duke of Edinburgh seems to belong not to history but to the world of Gilbert and Sullivan. A career sailor who certainly put to sea but never saw action on his way to the top, practically the only Englishman actually to have met the Mikado in person, he occupied rooms at Clarence House that could have served for a production of *Patience*. That he was not only an admirer of the Savoy Operas but a friend of Sir Arthur Sullivan should come as no surprise. Sullivan, who regarded Affie as one of his 'oldest and best friends', was a regular guest

at the Duke and Duchess's country house, Eastwell Park near Ashford in Kent, where the days – according to the season – would be spent shooting or butterfly hunting, and the evenings in musical parties.

The Duke was a passionate advocate of music education and a prime mover in the establishment of the Royal College of Music, which was opened by the Prince of Wales in 1883. Sullivan's intention to bequeath to him the manuscript score of one of his oratorios was frustrated by the Duke's death from cancer of the larynx at Coburg in July 1900.

Soon after the Duke of Edinburgh's funeral, his younger brother Prince Arthur learnt that the Duchess intended to give up Clarence House. Arthur wrote to his brother the Prince of Wales, hoping that 'as Affie's next brother you will consider that I have some claim – it is a very nice house and has a little bit of garden which is an immense advantage'. Against the Prince of Wales's protestations the Queen decided in favour of Prince Arthur, who had been from an early age her favourite son.

ARTHUR, DUKE OF CONNAUGHT AND STRATHEARN (1900–1942)

The third son of Queen Victoria and Prince Albert, Prince Arthur (1850–1942) was named after his godfather, the 81-year-old Duke of Wellington. The Prince was commissioned in the Royal Engineers in 1868. He was created Duke of Connaught and Strathearn and Earl of Sussex in 1874 and given his own country house, Bagshot Park, on the edge of Windsor Great Park. He replaced the existing house with a much larger one, which was almost complete by his marriage in July 1879 to Princess Louise Margaret, youngest daughter of Prince Frederick Charles of Prussia. The Duke's military career progressed quickly, and as major-general he commanded the 1st Guards Brigade with distinction at the Battle of Tel-el-Kebir in Egypt in 1882. The Duke and Duchess had three children: Margaret (b.1882), Arthur (b.1883) and Patricia (b.1886).

As an army officer, the Duke spent long periods overseas, and following his retirement he was appointed Governor-General of Canada, living there from 1911 to 1916. A year after his return the Duchess died from a chronic illness. The Duke continued to carry out official duties but with advancing age settled into a routine of spending each winter on the Riviera, returning to Bagshot and Clarence House for the summer. After his death in 1942, Clarence House was made available for the use of the War Organisation of the British Red Cross and Order of St John of Jerusalem for the duration of the war. The staff of the Foreign Relations Department maintained contact from Clarence House with British prisoners-of-war abroad, and administered the Red Cross Postal Message Scheme. In the summer of 1944 an exhibition was held in the garden to illustrate the daily life and living conditions of prisoners-of-war.

ABOVE LEFT
John Singer Sargent, *Arthur, Duke of Connaught*, oil on canvas, 1910.

ABOVE RIGHT
John Singer Sargent (1856–1925), *Louise, Duchess of Connaught*, oil on canvas, 1910.

RIGHT
The Duke of Connaught inspecting the Yeomen of the Guard in the garden of Clarence House.

PRINCESS ELIZABETH AND PHILIP, DUKE OF EDINBURGH (1949–1952)

BELOW

The Dining Room today, showing the Georgian dining table and 20 ladder-back chairs which were a wedding gift from the Royal Warrant Holders Association. Much of the furniture came in the form of wedding presents; the mahogany sideboard and four side tables were a present from Queen Mary, for whom they had been made in the 1890s. Chandeliers for the Drawing Rooms were presented by the Queen, while other members of the Royal Family gave a combined present in the form of a Hepplewhite bookcase for Princess Elizabeth's Sitting Room.

When Princess Elizabeth married Lieutenant Philip Mountbatten, RN, on 20 November 1947, she was living with her parents, King George VI and Queen Elizabeth, at Buckingham Palace. Several possible homes were considered for the newly married couple, now known as the Duke and Duchess of Edinburgh. As a London residence, Clarence House was the obvious choice but it needed complete refurbishment and, with wartime restrictions on building work still largely in force, progress was slow. The Duke and Duchess were given a suite of rooms at Buckingham Palace while Clarence House was being overhauled, and it was at the Palace on 14 November 1948 that their first child, Prince Charles, was born.

Work at Clarence House was completed early in 1949 and in June the Duke and Duchess moved in. The remarkable simplicity of the interior, once again without any gilding and entirely decorated in pale colours, was described by Christopher Hussey in a book published in 1949: 'a sunny, cheerful, happy house, appropriately spacious but reasonably compact, fit for a future Queen ... Yet there is also the modern note of simplicity.' The modern central heating and labour-saving kitchen equipment were admired in another book on the House by Marguerite Peacock, who observed that 'everything has been designed with a view to saving labour, for the Princess runs her home on one of the smallest staffs ever employed at a major London residence'.

Princess Anne was born at Clarence House in August 1950, a few weeks after the Duke of Edinburgh had been promoted to Lieutenant-Commander and appointed to his first command, the frigate HMS *Magpie*. For much of 1951 the King endured ill health, undergoing major surgery in September. His recovery was sufficient to allow the Duke and Duchess of Edinburgh to embark on their first foreign visit, to Canada and the United States, and in late January 1952 they set off on an intended tour of East Africa, Australia and New Zealand. News of the King's sudden death at the age of 56 on 6 February reached them in Kenya. With the Duchess's accession as Queen the royal couple moved to live once again in Buckingham Palace, while Clarence House was prepared for the accommodation of Queen Elizabeth The Queen Mother.

ABOVE

Philip de Laszlo (1869–1937), *HRH Princess Elizabeth of York*, oil on canvas, 1933. This portrait of the young Princess Elizabeth now hangs in the Morning Room.

OPPOSITE

Edward Halliday, *Maundy Thursday 1952*, 1952. This painting shows The Queen and The Duke of Edinburgh with Prince Charles and Princess Anne in the Sitting Room at Clarence House, soon after the accession.

RIGHT

A portrait of Queen Elizabeth The Queen Mother at Clarence House, by photographer Norman Parkinson, 1970.

QUEEN ELIZABETH THE QUEEN MOTHER (1953–2002)

Lady Elizabeth Angela Marguerite Bowes-Lyon was born on 4 August 1900, the ninth of the ten children of the Earl and Countess of Strathmore. Her father, the 14th Earl, had married in 1881 Nina, daughter of Archdeacon Charles Cavendish-Bentinck, a grandson of the 3rd Duke of Portland. The future Queen Elizabeth spent most of her childhood at St Paul's Walden Bury, her parents' house near Hitchin in Hertfordshire.

Lady Elizabeth Bowes-Lyon and Prince Albert of York, second son of the future King George V and Queen Mary, probably first met at a children's party when she was five and he was ten. Their courtship began around the time Prince Albert was created Duke of York, in 1920, and they were married in Westminster Abbey on 26 April 1923.

During the first years of their marriage the Duke and Duchess travelled extensively, touring East Africa in 1924 and making a six-month visit to Australia and New Zealand in 1927. In April 1926 their first child, the Princess Elizabeth, was born at 17 Bruton Street in Mayfair, which belonged to the Duchess's mother, the Countess of

Queen Elizabeth had long been an admirer of John's work when, in 1939, he asked to paint her portrait. The sittings took place in Buckingham Palace in June 1940 but the artist was overcome by shyness and, despite encouragement, failed to complete the picture. It remained in his studio until the last year of his life, when it was presented to Queen Elizabeth on the occasion of the launch of the liner SS *Northern Star*. Replying to a letter from the sitter in July 1961, the artist wrote of his reluctance to exhibit the picture in its unfinished state: 'but now that it hangs upon your wall, I am convinced that with all its faults, there is something there which is both true and lovable. I had really thought so all along but I have not dared to say so.'

LEFT
Augustus John,
OM, RA (1878–1961),
HM Queen Elizabeth,
oil on canvas, 1940.

Strathmore. On their return from Australia the Duke and Duchess and their daughter moved into 145 Piccadilly, and the King allowed them to have Birkhall near Balmoral in Scotland and Royal Lodge in Windsor Great Park as country houses. The Piccadilly house was destroyed in the war but Queen Elizabeth continued to use Birkhall and Royal Lodge until her death in 2002. The Duke and Duchess's second daughter, Princess Margaret Rose, was born at Glamis Castle in 1930.

The Abdication Crisis of 1936 brought the Duke and Duchess abruptly and unexpectedly to Buckingham Palace as King George VI and Queen Elizabeth. Queen Elizabeth's decision to remain in London throughout the Second World War, and the King's courage in fulfilling the intensely heavy duty of leadership that had been placed on him, made the Royal Family a powerful focus for national unity,

especially after Buckingham Palace itself was hit by German bombs in September 1940.

After King George VI's death at Sandringham in February 1952, Queen Elizabeth was granted the use of Clarence House for her lifetime, moving to live there with Princess Margaret in May 1953, shortly before the Coronation. She also purchased and restored an almost ruined sixteenth-century castle, the Castle of Mey, on the Pentland Firth in Caithness in the far north of Scotland, where she would usually spend the month of August.

During The Queen and Prince Philip's world tour of 1953–4, Queen Elizabeth carried out many of their official duties, receiving foreign ambassadors in audience and presiding over investitures for the distribution of honours. In subsequent years, all foreign heads of state called at Clarence House for tea in the afternoon of the first day of a state visit, and Queen Elizabeth attended the state banquet at Buckingham Palace on the second day; when state visitors stayed at Windsor, Queen Elizabeth would entertain them at Royal Lodge.

The atmosphere of Clarence House was derived not from its comparatively plain architecture and decoration, but from the way the rooms were furnished and hung with works of art acquired by Queen Elizabeth over her 60-year career as a collector and patron of artists. As John Cornforth has written:

Whereas some people (particularly those interested in decoration) see rooms as complete compositions, not liking individual objects to distract from the whole, and others concentrate on individual objects, with little eye for their relationship to one another or their setting (as can happen with collectors), at Clarence House several of the rooms seem to build up from separate compositions of pictures and objects, with flowers and plants also playing their part.

Walter Richard Sickert, ARA (1860–1942), *A Conversation Piece at Aintree*, oil on canvas, c.1927–30 (purchased in 1951). This painting is based on a photograph of King George V and his stud manager Major F.H.W. Featherstonhaugh that appeared in the News Chronicle on 25 March 1927. The artist, who often used news photographs as the basis for paintings at this time, inscribed the canvas 'By Courtesy of Topical Press'.

After Princess Margaret's marriage in 1960, Queen Elizabeth opened out two of the rooms on the ground floor of Clarence House to form the Garden Room, a large and sunlit room well suited to entertaining large groups of guests. When luncheons or evening receptions took place during the summer months, the rooms were filled with flowers and all the doors and windows on the south side of the House were opened, so that the House and the garden appeared as one continuous scene. These occasions, which continued into Queen Elizabeth's eleventh decade and were attended by an extraordinary cross-section of people, were characterised by a unique blend of grandeur and informality. Greeted in the porch by liveried footmen and led into the Morning

Claude Monet (1840–1926), *Study of Rocks, the Creuse: 'Le Bloc'*, oil on canvas, 1889 (purchased in 1945).

Room, visitors might first be struck by either a magnificent Monet landscape or a stack of pictures that had not yet found a place on the walls, or even perhaps a favourite tennis ball abandoned on a chair by one of Queen Elizabeth's corgis.

From 1970, when Queen Elizabeth celebrated her 70th birthday, until 2001, the Royal Family assembled at Clarence House every year on 4 August for what became a traditional birthday appearance, as well-wishers would crowd into Stable Yard Road to offer presents. In 1990 and 2000 these celebrations were extended; gala parades were organised in the Mall and on Horse Guards.

Following Queen Elizabeth's death at Royal Lodge on Easter Saturday, 30 March 2002, The Queen decided that Clarence House should become the London residence of His Royal Highness The Prince of Wales and of the Princes William and Harry.

BELOW
The Queen Mother with The Prince of Wales on Horse Guards Parade on 19 July 2000, for Her Majesty's 100th birthday celebration.

CHARLES, PRINCE OF WALES (2003–)

The Prince of Wales was born at Buckingham Palace on 14 November 1948 and moved to Clarence House with his parents in June the following year.

By the time of Queen Elizabeth's death in April 2002, more than 50 years had passed since the last major refurbishment of the House, and substantial works were required. The structural and related works included fire compartmentation, automatic fire detection, electrical rewiring, the renewal of lifts and kitchen appliances, the removal of asbestos, and redecoration. These were completed in less than a year, paid for with funds from the grant-in-aid for the maintenance of the occupied royal palaces. The cost of refurnishing the House and of

the restoration of the contents was met by The Prince of Wales personally. In 2004–05 His Royal Highness added the formal garden in front of the House in memory of Queen Elizabeth. It was laid out to his own design by members of The Prince's School of Traditional Arts.

LEFT
The formal garden in front of Clarence House was created in 2004–05 to a design by The Prince of Wales in memory of his grandmother.

LEFT
Their Royal Highnesses The Prince of Wales and The Duchess of Cornwall pose with their families at Windsor Castle, following their marriage on 9 April 2005; back row left to right, Prince Harry, Prince William, Tom and Laura Parker Bowles; front row left to right, The Duke of Edinburgh, The Queen and Major Bruce Shand, the Duchess's father.

Clarence House is The Prince of Wales's official residence as Heir to the Throne. Here he and The Duchess of Cornwall receive or entertain more than a thousand guests every year, many of them important visitors from the UK and overseas, or people connected with the work of The Prince of Wales's charitable foundations or with some of the 350 charitable organisations with whose work The Prince or The Duchess is involved. The ground-floor rooms of the House are used for official meetings and receptions, while the private living rooms are on the floor above, with bedrooms and other rooms for Prince Harry, together with their staff, on the upper two floors. Immediately on moving into the House, His Royal Highness decided that the ground-floor rooms should be opened to the public during the summer months when they are not in official use.

Tour of Clarence House

ENTRANCE HALL

Visitors approach the South Front through the gardens laid out in 2004–05 by HRH The Prince of Wales, to his own design, in memory of his grandmother, Queen Elizabeth The Queen Mother. The Doric portico leads to the Entrance Hall, both created for Alfred, Duke of Edinburgh in the 1870s, as part of the remodelling of the South Front by C.B Waller to form the main entrance façade.

RIGHT
The sundial in the new gardens in front of the House, with the façade of St James's Palace beyond.

ABOVE
Nicolas de Largillière (1656–1746), *Prince James Francis Edward (the 'Old Pretender') and his sister Princess Louisa Maria Teresa, c.*1695 (purchased in 1965 from the collection of Lord Elphinstone, Queen Elizabeth's brother-in-law).

LANCASTER ROOM

OPPOSITE

The Lancaster Room as it looks today, following redecoration and refurbishing for HRH The Prince of Wales.

BELOW RIGHT

Franz Xaver Winterhalter (1805–73), *The Presentation of King Louis-Philippe's Grandsons to Queen Victoria at the Château d'Eu, September 1845*, oil on canvas, 1845. The setting for this picture is the Galerie Victoria at the Château d'Eu in Normandy, where the French King intended to install a series of 30 specially commissioned pictures recording Queen Victoria's visit to France and his own to Windsor in 1844. The project was cut short by the revolution of 1848. The picture was purchased by Queen Elizabeth in 1947.

In the Duke of Clarence's time this, the first room opening off the Hall when entering from the South Front, was the Equerry's Room, and it has served all the subsequent occupants of the House as a waiting room for visitors. The name derives from a fund donated as a wedding present to The Princess Elizabeth and The Duke of Edinburgh by the people of Lancashire for the fitting-out of the House. The fund was used for the purchase of the chimneypiece, which came from a house in St Stephen's Green, Dublin, built by the 2nd Lord Brandon, and was subsequently in a house in Lowndes Square, Belgravia. To judge from the bunches of grapes carved on the central tablet, it must originally have been intended for a dining room.

LEFT

Norma Bull (1906–80), *Rescue at Knightsbridge by Heavy Rescue Party during a Raid: Flying Bomb Incident of 3.8.44*, watercolour, 1944.

There are seven watercolour views of Windsor Castle in the Lancaster Room, painted by John Piper in the early 1940s, with more in the Dining Room (see p. 51) and Hall. The series was commissioned from the artist at the suggestion of Sir Kenneth Clark, Director of the National Gallery and Surveyor of The King's Pictures, after Queen Elizabeth had visited an exhibition of the work of the 'Recording Britain' project. It was intended as a record of the Castle in case of war damage.

ABOVE

Pietro Annigoni (1910–88), *HRH Prince Philip, Duke of Edinburgh*, study in black chalk, 1962.

MORNING ROOM

ABOVE
The Morning Room.

RIGHT
Detail of the ceiling
plasterwork showing
Queen Elizabeth's crown.

In Nash's original design for the Duke of Clarence's house, this was the breakfast room. The large window looking into the garden to the south was introduced by the Duchess of Kent around 1841, while in Alfred, Duke of Edinburgh's time the room was elaborately redecorated in the 'Aesthetic' style with painted and stencilled decoration. Between 1949 and 1952, when it

served as The Duke of Edinburgh's study, the walls were panelled in pale Canadian maple (see p. 19). Queen Elizabeth inserted the double doors at the northern end and commissioned a new plaster ceiling with crowns and Garter badges in relief, at the same time introducing the chimneypiece and flanking display niches.

BELOW
Walter Richard Sickert,
ARA (1893–1964) *A Lady
in a Pink Ballgown*, 1941
(purchased in 1941).

BELOW
Augustus John, OM, RA (1878–1961), *When Homer
Nods: Portrait of George Bernard Shaw*, oil on canvas,
1915. One of three portraits painted during the same
sequence of sittings, when both artist and sitter were
staying at Castle Coole in the west of Ireland as guests
of Lady Gregory. The sittings were lengthy and Shaw
fell asleep before this version was complete
(purchased in 1938).

LEFT
Year-going longcase equation
clock by Thomas Tompion
(1639–1713), made for
William III. The outer, 24-hour dial
(marked 'Apparent Time') moves both
backwards and forwards to
record against the fixed inner dial
(marked 'Mean Time'). The
complex mechanism, of which
this is thought to be the earliest
surviving example by Tompion,
was intended to overcome the
seasonal variations in the time as
measured by the sun.

ABOVE
Sir Herbert James Gunn,
RA (1893–1964),
HM Queen Elizabeth,
1945, study for the portrait
commissioned by the
Middle Temple, in which
Her Majesty is portrayed
as Royal Bencher
(presented by the artist
in 1945).

LIBRARY

After Ludwig
Schwanthaler (1802–48),
four gilt-bronze statuettes
of rulers of Bavaria.
Part of a set of 12
reductions of statues
made for the Thronsaal
of the Munich Residenz,
presented to
Queen Victoria by
Prince Albert on her
birthday in 1843. The
remainder of the set is
in the Dining Room
and Lancaster Room.

The Library, looking
towards the Dining Room
through one of the new
double doors that
Queen Elizabeth
The Queen Mother
had installed to link the
Dining Room, Library
and Morning Room.

As designed by Nash, this was the
Entrance Hall to the House from the
double portico in Stable Yard Road (see plan
on p. 12). The door was blocked in the
Duchess of Kent's time, when the entrance
was moved to its present position to allow
more discreet access. Princess Elizabeth and
The Duke of Edinburgh fitted the room
with bookshelves (now replaced by free-
standing bookcases). Queen Elizabeth used
it for dining with small numbers of guests,
and opened a new doorway from this room
through into the Hall.

Savely Sorine (1887–1953),
HRH The Duchess of York,
watercolour, 1923.
This portrait shows
Queen Elizabeth
The Queen Mother before
the Abdication Crisis of
1936, when she was still
Duchess of York.

LEFT
The Dining Room, detail showing the table prepared for a formal occasion.

BELOW
This large eighteenth-century Chinese parade jar and cover on an English giltwood stand is displayed in the Dining Room.

DINING ROOM

This room has always served as the Dining Room. The Duchess of Kent introduced gilding to the mouldings, in an attempt to lighten a naturally rather dark room, while the Adam-style ceiling enrichments in papier-mâché composition are thought to date from the Duke of Connaught's occupation in the early 1900s. The present 'Pompeian' scheme of decoration was carried out under the direction of Robert Kime during the recent refurbishment of the House.

LEFT
Sir Edwin Landseer
(1803–73), *Hector, Nero
and Dash with the Parrot,
Lory*, oil on canvas, 1838.
This was painted for
Queen Victoria; Dash, a
cavalier spaniel, belonged
to the Queen from 1833
until his death in 1840.
The greyhound Nero may
have belonged to the
Duchess of Kent, and the
rare Scottish deerhound
Hector had been given to
the Queen (then Princess)
in 1835. The Lory was
a present from her
uncle Duke Ernest I of
Saxe-Coburg and Gotha
in 1836.

RIGHT
Augustine Courtauld
(1685/6–1751), cup and
cover with twisted serpent
handles, 1738, later
engraved with the coronet
and initials of Augustus
Frederick, Duke of Sussex
(purchased in 1947).

ABOVE
David Willaume
(1658–1741), sideboard
dish and ewer engraved
with the arms of the
Bowes family, 1718.

JOHN PIPER AT WINDSOR CASTLE

BELOW
John Piper, CH (1903–92), *The Quadrangle at Windsor Castle looking towards the Round Tower*, watercolour, gouache, pen and black ink, 1942.

In 1941 the artist wrote to John Betjeman: 'I follow unworthily in the footsteps of Paul Sandby, who did two hundred watercolours for George III, which I am instructed to look at earnestly before starting.' In total there are 14 watercolour views of Windsor by Piper in the Dining Room, and more in the Lancaster Room and the Hall. The series was

commissioned from the artist at the suggestion of Sir Kenneth Clark, Director of the National Gallery and Surveyor of The King's Pictures, after Queen Elizabeth had visited an exhibition of the work of the 'Recording Britain' project. It was intended as a record of the Castle in case of war damage.

BELOW
John Piper, CH (1903–92), *The Quadrangle from Engine Court, Windsor Castle*, watercolour, gouache, pen and black ink, 1942.

RIGHT
John Piper, CH (1903–92), *The Round Tower from the roof of St George's Chapel, Windsor Castle*, watercolour, gouache, pen and black ink, 1942.

LEFT
John Piper, CH (1903–92), *The North Terrace and Winchester Tower, Windsor Castle*, watercolour, gouache, pen and black ink, 1942.

Designed by John Nash as a corridor of communication between the principal rooms on the ground floor, with another corridor of the same dimensions serving the same purpose on the floor above, this became the principal access route to the House after the Duchess of Kent moved the main entrance from the west side to the south end of the corridor (see p. 12). The present ceiling was introduced for Princess Elizabeth and The Duke of Edinburgh after the 'Elizabethan' ceiling designed for Alfred, Duke of Edinburgh, was found to be unsound.

RIGHT
British School,
*Lady Bowes, wife of
Sir Thomas Bowes, c.*1620
(purchased in 1963).

ABOVE
The Hall, showing
four of the set of 12
eighteenth-century walnut
dining chairs.

RIGHT
Pieces from the 'King of
Hanover' service of Worcester
porcelain, c.1795. The painted
decoration by John Pennington
reproduces compositions by Sir
Joshua Reynolds, Angelica
Kauffmann and other artists.

HORSE CORRIDOR

This corridor is part of the extension of the House made for Alfred, Duke of Edinburgh, by Waller & Sons in the mid-1870s (see p.14). It is named for the large collection of sporting pictures assembled by Queen Elizabeth, which celebrate her own victories on the turf along with those of the most successful owner and breeder of the Bowes family, John Bowes (1811–85).

RIGHT
Late seventeenth-century red and black lacquer secretaire, possibly German.

BELOW
The Garden Room, showing Jakob Bogdani (d.1720), *Birds in a Landscape*, *c.*1708–10, and the tapestry *Mahommed Ali's Massacre of the Mamelukes at Cairo*.

This room was created by Queen Elizabeth from two rooms which formed part of the 1870s extension. The larger of the two (towards the chimneypiece) was Princess Margaret's sitting room, when she lived here before her marriage in 1960, and the smaller room was for the use of her lady-in-waiting.

The tapestry which dominates the end wall is *Mahommed Ali's Massacre of the Mamelukes at Cairo*, French (Gobelins Manufactory), after Horace Vernet (1789–1863). It was shown at the Great Exhibition of 1851 and subsequently presented to Queen Victoria by Emperor Napoleon III. The two pictures by the Hungarian-born painter Jakob Bogdani (d.1720), both entitled *Birds in a Landscape*, *c.*1708–10, depict birds from the aviary established at Windsor by

Admiral George Churchill, brother of the Duke of Marlborough. Bogdani was settled in London by 1691 and worked for William III and Queen Anne. These two paintings were purchased by Queen Anne from Churchill's executors after his death in 1710.

OPPOSITE
The Garden Room.

Duke of Clarence

The name is derived from the honour of Clare in Suffolk (an honour is the estate of a tenant-in-chief of the Crown). The title was first conferred on Lionel of Antwerp, third son of Edward III, in 1362. It was subsequently held from 1412 by Thomas, second son of Henry IV, and from 1461 by George, brother of Edward IV, who was murdered at the Tower of London in 1478, supposedly by drowning in a butt of Malmsey wine. Prince William Henry, later William IV, held the title between 1789 and his accession in 1830. The most recent holder was Prince Albert Victor, grandson of Queen Victoria, who was created Duke of Clarence and Avondale in 1890, two years before his death.

Duke of Connaught

Originally a royal earldom conferred on Prince William Henry, Duke of Gloucester and Edinburgh, brother of George III, as a subsidiary title in 1764, this became a royal dukedom in 1874 when Prince Arthur, third son of Queen Victoria, was created Duke of Connaught and Strathearn. He was succeeded by his grandson Alastair, Earl of Macduff, in 1942, who died in the following year, whereupon the Connaught title became extinct.

Duke of Edinburgh

Prince Frederick Louis, eldest son of George, Prince of Wales (later George II), was created Duke of Edinburgh in 1726. He died in 1751 and his son George, Prince of Wales, 2nd Duke of Edinburgh, eventually succeeded to the throne as George III in 1760. In 1764 George III

conferred the title on his brother William Henry, Duke of Gloucester and Edinburgh, on the death of whose son, also William, in 1834 the title became extinct. In 1866 Queen Victoria created her second son, Prince Alfred, Duke of Edinburgh, the title becoming extinct once again on his death in 1900. It was revived by King George VI when he conferred the dukedom on his son-in-law, Lieutenant Philip Mountbatten, RN, on the day of his marriage to Princess Elizabeth, 20 November 1947.